Notes From The In-Between

By Noelle Cope

Book Cover by Noelle Cope Cover Model Noelle Cope
Illustrations by Noelle Cope Illustrations Model Noelle Cope
Author photo by C.C. Cope

ISBN: 979-8-218-96955-4

First Edition 2024

10 9 8 7 6 5 4 3 2

Index

Trigger Warning

This book is themed around recovering from abuse and contains poems focusing on the themes of emotional abuse, sexual violence and the experience of life with C-PTSD.

Fellow survivors are advised to prioritize self care and wellness while reading. Please seek professional help if needed.

Sexual Abuse Hotline for U.S. Readers
RAINN 1-800-656-4673

Introduction

You hold a collection of poems written within a three-year span of my life. This is a time in writing often referred to as the " In- Betweens" a simplistic, almost childlike way of trying to summarize how trauma altered the way I perceived the world and myself.

Since early childhood, writing has been my escape, my best friend, my greatest love, and my therapy. During the time leading up to, then during and after the "In-Between", I wrote hundreds of poems without intending to share them publicly.

Many parts of my experience and story have been omitted. It would be impossible and exhausting to even attempt such a lengthy recount in its entirety. However, each poem included in this collection was carefully (painstakingly) selected and arranged to best share an intimate look into this experience, free of stigma, stereotypes, and statistics.

Essentially, these are my field notes.

So with that... Let us enter the In-Between...

No one warns you of the journey many of us go on. Even if they do they inevitably leave out so much.

There is always much more to this:

The year(s) spent wandering in the space between the sun and the moon. The feeling of those seconds, hours, days and months living neither in light nor darkness; the In-Between.

In the In-Between, people adopt masks often blurring the lines between friend and foe.

Here the only way out is in.

To leave the space between life and death - before and after.

No stone or corner of self can be overlooked if you truly wish to return to life free from the ghost you now know yourself to be.

For those who have not to taken this journey may the following words serve as a roadmap to help understand this experience from the inside out.

For those who are on the other-side may you find comfort in the shared experience. The reminder that you will always have tender arms to return to. There is love.

For those still lost in the In-Between may this be the guide I wish I had. You'll survive this.

Case Study 01:
New Discoveries

(Who I was before)
The rules of the game only exist
for those who play the game.

What if the princess was the dragon guarding the tower all along?

I think that is me.
Deep down I always knew I was a dragon
I was born breathing fire
and scared all the nurses
my poor mother warned of my bad behavior
an hour after my arrival.

I had a taste for flight
and no time to waste
passion was my birth right.

Still others thought of me as doe or dove
so soft,
so sweet,
so eager to be the healer
in the hospital rooms
I wander in childhood
but still I knew the flip side of my own coin
behind the golden brown eyes and cupid bow lips.

Perhaps, a little too comfortable with death
perhaps, more enlightened than others
fire and fury always cut through me
like an icy mountain pass,
I am the winter's dragon
guarding my keep
letting few in as I gather my treasures,
finding new ways to let out the steam
that singes my breath.

Unexpectedly
between dreams
and waking
it floats in around me

"Jó reggelt kívánok"
The smell of coffee all around
as the sound of mother tongue
flows between Anya and Nagymama.

Perhaps, there in the distance
a call from Nagypapa
will fill the space
as breakfast is made.

My little hands step up
for my task
setting out the
sö and Paprika
then I ask help
from bigger hands
to pour out the tej.

All around me,
I feel the hum of the language
solidifying in my bones
a gentle roaring rhythmic
sound that would define
the feeling of home
throughout my past, present, and future.

Tapping,
humming,
wiggling,
swaying,
side to side.

Eyes always searching
this curiosity never contained
a mind who's gears know no other way to spin.

I was made in the realm of reaching.

Always wanting to explore things near and far
my specialty - the human heart.

Nowhere
have I found
a more curious object
than that beating thing
and all it dares to create.

It feels like learning to walk for the first time
wobbly,
unsteady,
courageous.

I've been watching and learning
my whole life up until now

I wanna try for myself
no longer hide myself away
keeping these creations of mine
hidden where it's safe

Maybe I'm not ready to walk yet
but I'm ready to fall down while I try
making something new out of it
I learn on the way down.

Knew since birth
why small gestures
bring the biggest joys
always liked swinging in silence
watching the clear blue sky
dreaming of flight
while birds sing
teaching me their ways.

There is rare beauty to just feeling
the wind and my breath
knowing they are the same.
I always liked the silence
teaching me how to sing.

Other days, I learn
from the dying people
how to star gaze the right way
seeing the whole universe -
                              the light that lies beyond
                                    the place maybe they will
                                          explore next.

I don't know much about God
but I know the mountains and the river
and the deer and baby bears,
I know the rocks I climb that skin my knee
and the sound snow makes when it falls.
I like story books and slow movies
because it feels like they know the secret
to life that only me and the dying do.

I'm feeling hopeful

I'm hopeful about
all the progress I'm making.

I know that lows will keep coming
with the highs
but I'm confident
in my abilities to ride
both elements with grace

I trust the person
I know me to be.

Small steps
forward
almost invisible
on paper.

Still I move forward
day by day,
celebrating each small victory,
even when I stumble.

I could fit the whole world
in my hand -
if I wanted to.

But that would be rather boring.

So I'm playing hide and seek with the world
setting off to explore it
in places near and far.
But no matter how many miles or oceans I cross
I find the little strings only I can see.

A tree that looks like mine,
a smell that belongs to my nagymama,
a song that my father plays,
a movie my mother gave me.

All over the world and in all these places
pieces of where I came from
and where I'm going meld together
crafting the story of my life as I'm writing it.

I could fit the whole world
in my hand
if I wanted to
but I'd rather try to
fit it on the page.

I am a restless creature by nature
who was taught to fear
my wondering ways

Who was force fed anxiety
to keep me in line

All my intrusive thoughts,
come to me in voices that
are not my own.

Redirects I was taught
in order to make me moldable,
to tame my spirit
that wished to live
outside the lines they
wanted to paint me in.

I wonder how much of
this adult life
I will spend
trying to get back to
my wondering wild ways ?

I remember this place
though I've never been here before
these words come back to me
as if I've spoken them many times
in a memory.

I feel myself but not as I am now
but as someone I used to be.

A life and body hidden behind a waterfall.

There are moments
when I can make it out
and times during these new days
when I find my way home through
this " New City" without a map
or known memory.

I think it's hot in Texas.
You drive with your AC blasting,
radio turned low,
hat on the passenger seat.

You aren't the type to look back often,
blue eyes forever on the horizon line,
kinda guy.

But maybe from time to time
you'll catch a glimpse of something
or someone and remember
your California days.

The same way even 7 years later,
I meet another scorpio with your birthday,
and recall the fire you started
back in the City Of Angels.

Summer finds me at last,
sneaking up on me out of nowhere
even if my calendar tried to warn me.

In spite of myself,
I welcome the soft touch
and warm embrace of summer's sun
and breezy ways.

The way she says
it's not lazy
to loosen my grip.

It will never
no matter what you do
change.

Someday,
soon you'll find yourself
on the street corner
with someone you once knew.

You'll realize they haven't gotten better
in fact they have gotten worse -
before you know it
you'll hear yourself say
"Sending light and love"
Then be on your way, again.

My thoughts are powerful
but I doubt them often
when met with other's
louder thoughts.

Persuaded by the answers they claim to hold
reflected in their "success"
I feel far more inclined to buy what they are selling
than follow my own understanding of life.

      - This is how I get into trouble

When I demand,
despite other's protest,
the solitary space
I know is needed to hear myself
most clearly
I find the answers to take away
the banging in my body
that has started to sound
like a warning bell.

In the place where only my voice is heard
I see answers needed
though unconventional
but in this place I no longer
fear what I know to be true.

- This is how I get out of trouble

Rich man this
Poor man that

Ain't no man
(last time I checked)

So what does any of this matter ?

Just give me some bread, fruit, and a roof.

A little space to create
and create some more.

Money holds no meaning
except for division,
money is only a distraction
from the connection I'm drafting.

Money could never buy
this feeling I'm crafting.

Still we need it - I need it.

No way through it
no way around it
I already tried and tried and tired.

So a deal with money should be made
even if I don't want to play
the Rich man - Poor man games.

No One In LA Has A job

Just look around at
the weeknight romps till 6am
acting classes at 2pm
the aisles of Nordstrom packed all hours all day
- and night

The rules need not apply to the
freshly made faces here
yet…
We all play the same game
of guessing where all this money comes from?

Social media holds no clues
an endless cycle of updates hiding the trails
to blur the secret class system
we all signed up for
somewhere along the way.

A city run by influencers,
who fake being socialites,
while socialites fake being artists along side the nepo babies,
and both live in hopes of finding the meaning
money couldn't buy them.

As the real artists drown
hoping no one sees
behind the curtain of creation.

The curtain that would reveal
the day job they pray never takes root
And becomes their "identity"

Only one rare group ever longs for work

Those who are socially denied the chance.
The former child actors watch on
debating if
there is a job out there for them
that won't inspire pity.

So, they romanticize the grind
and what it must be like
to not pay mommy's bills.
No one in LA has a job
and that's how it is and will always stay
No one "works" in LA.

Peach juice drips down
winding it's way in little trails
down to my elbow.

Soon,
so soon.
Night shall fall
the music will play
and as if in a trance I'll sway.

Finding some new stranger to amuse,
and have a little fun
till it's time to leave
and I feel rather empty
for doing it at all.

I'll rise and repeat this the next day
and the day after,
and perhaps the day after that,
till summer ends,
and my skin has grown soft and golden
from the sun
and still ripe peaches drip
down upon my wrist
as if summer will last
till the hill sides burn.

Is it normal to think of my loved one's lives
after I die?

It's become normal for me.

I spend so much time worried that
no matter how many
photos I take,
voice mails I leave,
cards I write,
paintings I paint,
poems I share

That when I die they will never feel like
there are enough pieces of me
to fill the gap I left.

I'm scared of being missed
and being grieved
and being so dead
I can't do anything about it.

I spend so much time creating with this feeling that the hour glass is always
so close to running out

And I still haven't written every word I could
or left it in a place where someone can feel
like I found them again
when they needed me most.

I'm so afraid of my own loneliness
I can't sleep over the idea
that someday, someone will be lonely
because I'm not coming back.

Once I could call all the shots
before they were fired
knew what the world wanted next
before they did.

Could pull beauty out of thin air
never had to try

Life hacked me down
in the ways only
growing up can.

It chews a girl up
and spits her out.

Now I'm playing catch up
to play the game
I invented when I was 15
as my 30s rocket towards me

threatening to squish
what's left of
my former
gifted self.

It's not what
I wished for
but maybe
it's something
more.

A detour leading to
a treasure
beyond that
which others
tell me
to desire.

The midnight quiet
wraps me up
around me pours out
the gentle secrets
only I am meant to know.

This life is a puzzle
one made just for me
only someone forgot to give me
the box with the picture
or the cryptic key.

So I'm building it shape by shape,
piece by piece,
seeing the picture that is
my place in this mess.

Humming,
feet taping,
keeping time
to a song only I can hear.

There is a beat building
to the rhythm of my heart,

I feel it pulsing through me.

I know my place
and I feel myself growing to meet it.

The power that once lay dormant
would like to make its return
with me as it's catalyst.

It's coming
and
it's coming soon

A tidal wave only I will feel,
the earthquake that will shake only me,
the wild fire that only I will burn in.

I'm ready -
but can you ever be ready?
Yes and no.

How do you prepare for the unknown?
I don't think you can.

You can guess and try to cover
every base, I suppose.

I know what's coming will knock me down
But I'll get up.

Case Study 02: Chaos

Sometimes someone comes into your life
With the singular mission :
To set it all on fire

The Siren

There is a hum
within all of me
a tune my body has played
for as long as it has been a body.

This tune has scored
my every moment
waking and sleeping,
rising and falling,
in fight and in serenity.

I never wondered where this secret song
came from till I heard it cascade off your lips
that night under the stars laying in the grass
haunted by the ghosts of our idols.

Now I lie in bed
your song hanging all around

and click my heels together
one... two... three
times

hoping it will keep
bringing me to you.

Crept up on me
like an ant on a sugar cube
wound around my ankles like a hungry kitten
sang to me like a siren to a lost sailor
wrapped me in your arms like the unexpected
lover I'd spent my life looking for.

I think you are my best friend
but I don't want to tell my best friend that -
I don't want to hurt her feelings.

But you are *the best...*
maybe that's it
maybe, it's not even that you are my best friend
it's even more than that
but I like saying best friend
because it means
I'm a part of this, too.

Saying you are the best means
I could just be your admirer -

But to say you are my best friend means
that I know you
and better yet
you know me.

Which is true
because I've told you things
I've never told anyone
yet it still feels like there is
so much more to say.

I've never wanted anyone to
know all of me
before I met you.

I have something she wants,
and that something is you.

She used to like me
till she saw your hand on mine
I don't think she thinks of me
as a friend anymore
and I don't really know why.

I didn't ask you to be mine
but you came here
and stayed all the same.

You are trouble.
My kind of trouble.

What they label as pretentious
I know to be sincerity,
where others feel a cold shoulder
I feel serenity
where others see mystery
I see thoughtfulness.

They tell me *"never date an actor."*
They warn me *"never fall for a music man."*

But they don't see how
your brown eyes call to me
with a warmth only I can recognize.

Each step of this tango
is too familiar
a dance I've already danced
with 3 before you.

I know neither of us can say yes,
but neither of us want to say no.

Somewhere deep down
some part of you knows

I'm your kind of trouble too.

I like being a wild thing
too much for this risk
but still I can't seem to say no.

So with old world cards laid between us
your chin resting on the table
I tell you the rules
so I can have my cake and eat it too.

You agree and it starts,
first a bill you won't let me read that
ends with luxury white sheets
and Friends on TV.

So I place a new rule :
No more money

And into the purple haze we enter,
I try to tell myself I'm still in control,
when you make it clear
whisking me away at dusk
and returning me at dawn
are part of your terms
for our unique contract.

But this sleeping beauty story has a bite,
I'm too wrapped up in it to call out
maybe,
because I don't actually want to give it up.

A wild thing never wants to admit
when she is losing control
and finds herself becoming
someone's lap cat.

Old Hollywood house
rare November bite in the air

"No one's been over yet"

The boxes hadn't even arrived
but you wanted me.

So I swallowed my fear
and clung to the lie
that love hadn't already found us.

Pretended I wasn't here
feeling my treacherous heart
ignoring the haunted, paranormal air
and each flashing warning sign.

Because deep down I knew
any room would be home for me
if you were in it.

He tracks the stars
I light the candles
cards are pulled
secrets are shared
we hold close to the wisdom
ancestors slip through the veil
and promise to be each other's
protector.

"*Baby, your eyes are too big*"
your laughter
shaking my body
that rests against your chest.

"You like my big eyes"
I whisper like smoke.

You purse your lips
so I give them a kiss.

"I like your stupid face"
I concede as you pull away
eyes open at last.

"*I like your face but I wouldn't call it stupid*"
You say drinking me in again

We kiss once more,
then head for the road,
you, singing to yourself
a fairy tale melody
while I pray we get lost
looking for Ventura boulevard.

Would it be alright if I keep marveling
at your mind?
Because I don't think I've ever met any like it.
I want to know all the things you have to share.

Can you keep knowing me as well as I know
myself?
Because it feels so nice to be known.

Could you please keep being
too tender
and
thoughtful
and
somehow always knowing
when is the right time to talk about
all the things I try to hide?
It's nice to not have to live in the dark
of what's happening all the time.

Can I sit in the warmth of your silence ?
There is such a familiarity to the way you don't
need to always speak.
It reminds me of me.
And how I don't always need words to share
in the moment.

And lastly -

can we please always prioritize naps
above all else?
Mostly, because I still can't figure out if I like
being the little spoon -
or the big spoon more.

Soft amber light pours in
through the white tulle curtains
that like a dream frame the windows.

Light shines golden off his skin
black tank pulled tight
suddenly making this game of playing house
feel all the more delicious.

A man's man,
with a poet's soul,
eyes that wound me
a face that always leaves me breathless.

Yes, I'll be your playmate
just don't ever stop playing
I long to whisper
as he leans in closer
once more.

Soft steps,
tender touch,
never could throw a ball hard enough

I like fragile things
I am a fragile thing

Taking care
watching each moment,
ensuring nothing can shatter this
dream I never want to end

I'll be over protective
watching my every breath
make sure this can't be broken
because I like you

      Because
            I'm afraid
                  surely soon
                        I will love you.

Words tumble out
Softly, upon the pillow case
A growing warmth
Fills this space,
Hanging in the air,
Invisible wind chimes,
That live somewhere in our chest,
Sound out as the distance
Between you and me and me and you
Grows smaller,
           smaller,
                smaller.

                - Is this love?

Small rush
murmurs only moments ago
bringing us against each other.

Now at ease
his eyes playfully
hopefully, meet mine
I should be used to this by now.

The way he looks at me in
a crowded room
when no one else is looking

I feel it.

The flush of it on my face
then the tidal wave of that feeling
so familiar
Yet…

It still sends a thrill through me…

Home.

My chosen home for this life
and maybe
so many before.

He isn't one for romantic moments or gestures.
But it's okay I'm not always good at knowing how to accept them, anyway.

He grew up thinking the best way he could love was through sharing his wealth.
I grew up thinking the best way to love was to let yourself be needed by another.

But I won't let him spend his money on me because then I feel guilty.
A poor girl never takes what she can't payback.
It's the only way to not lose her power;
A man betrayed never lets himself need someone because of the shame he feels when that someone lets him down. Again.

Together we are kinda mismatched.
learning as we go.
How to expand and refine our own limits in love.
Perhaps, that's why it was so easy to fall right in step side by side with each other.

I am alive.

In a way I've never been before
both soaring far above the atmosphere
and sinking deep down into the earth.

With each touch I
feel something divine
I feel as if I have become
the universe all around.

You and I are now it's
only remaining inhabitants

The illusion of our game
finally stripped away
taking the world
as we knew it
with it.

We always have a choice.
Except for me when it comes to you.
Never once were you
an option, a choice, or a question.

I know destiny was holding me captive
when our paths crossed
my fate was sealed before our eyes locked
well before my first breath was taken

My fate was sealed when the universe
made me for you.

I always had wavering faith
till I met with fate
fate has brown eyes and a wide smile
with imperfect teeth
his walk is lop-sided
and his hair always
forms in perfect curls.

Seeing fate was like seeing the earth from space
a profound moment
with meaning so deep
I know my simple mind
could never fully grasp what
I experienced that day.
All I knew was at last
I was home in the universe
and finally everything made sense
when I looked into his eyes a second time.

I know my love for you
would scare you
for while your life has asked much of you
it has given you little experience with
how to love tenderly.

While, I am no master,
I have often experienced
the fullness of love.

I know not how to fear the joy of finding
someone who feels like home
in the ways you do.

The love I hold for you is patient
as old as time and the stars themselves
there is no need to rush.

So slowly I love you
piece by piece
till you are ready
to love me without fear.

I love the routine.
God I used to hate routines.
But with us it feels so magical.

On the good days
the days when you are doing better and
able to be here with me, mentally,
are so special to me.

I understand the days when you can't
You barely speak and everything I do reminds you
of someone you no longer like very much.

Or you get so busy with all the other things
you'll walk in the room
And be shocked to see me where you left me,
Even though I've been here for two nights now.

I know I just need to give you time and then all this will be better.
We are learning together.
I'm learning not to be afraid
And trust you with
All the breakable parts of me.

Which is why our routine is so special.
It tastes like the future,
The other side of this.

Inside jokes and tv shows,
Shared deserts and pillow fights,
Kisses and cuddles,
Before bed I love yous
And 2 am I love yous
Morning I love yous
And running out the door kisses.

I love our routine
because I want to stay
and have reason to.
I love to believe
that I can weather the storms in your head.

Like looking for sea glass,
I focus my eyes on all the beautiful bits,
I still see the imperfections clear as day
but willingly I look away.

I know you are growing to do the same with me
for the first time maybe
as the seasons pass
we shall both learn it's safe to love
and all our rough edges will be rubbed smooth.

You threw them out
like coins in the well

I caught and gathered each one
memorizing it just so

Hoping that someday
I'd know all of you.

Be as close to you
as I am to me.

For I love you
so easily
love you more
than the stars and the seas
and everything in between.

I wonder how long
we will play
this secret game.

I'm not complaining
I'm just curious.

Wondering what is next ...

In this game of me doing as he asks
while he builds the plan.
Lays the ground work for the future he keeps
telling me
He wants us to have.

I'm still not so sure
if it's really possible.
But maybe it's better this way
if I'm the skeptic
and he is the believer.

Maybe, it's better if we take it slow
and once his pride for me has grown
then we can start to live out the plans he
claims to be enacting.

Maybe, then I won't be a
miscellaneous secret.

To love you
feels like driving
down a dark road
in the dead of night
no moon hangs.
The stars too dim
to show me the way
so with headlights alone
I take it turn by turn
and pray that dawn finds me
before the next cliff's edge.

Effortless Comparisons

She is effortless in all the ways I am not.
I can't replace her.
And you don't know it
but that's what you're asking me to do.
To fill the void she left behind.
I wasn't given the life to grant me that.

She is the girl we dream to be: I am the girl we fear to end up like.
She is praised as elegant: I am belittled as strong.
And no amount of time, space, or wishes in candle flames
is gonna alter me to be more like her.
In all the places her life has been easy, mine has been hard-
and I know she has her own battle scars, but hers are hidden behind beauty,
luck, and some other stuff.

I've fought my own battles and I've fought to win them
I gained confidence because I thought at least I was loved- only to
learn all the bricks they used to build me up were the ones
they threw to ensure they'd shattered me.

For if I am not loved, and I am not beautiful, and I am not smart...
Then what am I? Who am I?

How do I fill a space that was never meant for me?
How do we lie and call it destiny
when destiny has always betrayed me?
I live here with you on borrowed time
But why? For what?
For your growing resentment of me
to help erase the pain of losing her.

I was not seen as a strange curious thing.
He did not look upon me
as if I lived behind glass.

While so many drew near only for
their own satisfaction at being near
something deemed so unique
he sat beside me
as if my presence was
as mundane as oxygen.

I was no longer a zoo creature
or a mannequin on display
I was simply me.

Standing at the crossroads
of being a girl growing
into a woman.

I mistook his lack of seeing me as novelty
to be an understanding.
A deep knowing from him of just who I was.

I was mistaken.

For while I was never a strange curiosity
a luxury to be marched around
for him I was much more akin
to a house plant,
he soon forgot to water.

Sometimes when he talks about his dog
I think he wishes she was already dead.

Am I the only one who can hear it ?

The way he blames his neglectful ways on a puppy who dared to lived to 8?

Maybe that's why I loved her so much when he wasn't around.

We were two strays he'd brought home
because he thought he should,
two sets of big brown eyes he thought
would make him the man he wanted to be
and then forgot about once people weren't there
to praise him for being so good to us
because he never was.

Sometimes, when he talks to me
I know he wishes I was already gone
because he so openly resents me.

I wonder if being with him is killing her
the way it's slowly killing me.

I sometimes dream of saving her
but maybe its because
I secretly dream about saving me.

Magic Thing To Do

I always wanted to believe in magic
ordinary or extraordinary,
life would be better if
life was more than I had known.

One hot summer's day I met you
and now I had something to believe in.

Loving you was such a magical thing to do.

All magic -
I've come to learn -
is a double edge sword.

Your point of pain
always found its mark
easily cutting me open
and cutting me up.

Still I worshiped you
as only a believer can do.

Till your blade
found a mark too
deep for even you.
And my fantasies
slowly shifted
from dreams of
earning your love
to visions of what a life
free from this pain
would be like -

If I could just remove
your venom from my heart
walk away from you -

- If only to prove I could -

It tasted sweet to imagine
each night
that I could
shatter this as easily
As you shatter me.

But I never do it
because loving you is
such a magical thing to do.

Fool's Game

He brings out the sadness in me.

I think he is trying to love me
but I've never really been able to tell
I know I love him but he never seems to want my love
most of the time if I sit in the silence
all of this feels like wishful thinking,
I'm too smart to follow blindly,
too loyal to just speak
so I'll try my best to shrink.

To stay small,
stay safe,
and stay beside him.

I try to hide the growing storm
that I have now become
a vortex that sucks all in
and gives none back.

A fear of so many things that all bear his face.

I always lie to myself that if I can just make it to tomorrow,
I can make it last.
That flowers will bloom within me again
and he'll find the love for me that's been misplaced.

It's a fools game.
But aren't we all fools for love...
at least once ?

Case Study 03:
Heart Break

The love we hold for another can't always keep us safe
from them.
And in the aftermath of such betrayal
It can feel as if our existence is scrambled.

I tried to keep you off the page
like I tried to keep you
out of my heart
but somehow
I still find your shadows
tucked in every word on
the blank pages I fill.

And your finger prints
in every nightmare that wakes me.

I am losing my way again
wanting to play games
for all to see again.

This only happens when you come around.
Setting about to make me unsure
helping to ensure I hate this town.

This loss of control
throw limb over limb
tumbling through space.

Only you make me feel
like I am no longer the
writer of my own story.

I'm scared -
Scared that you've taken away the pen
and I'm about to lose my way again.

Once it felt as if we were
falling into one another
that you were the oak
and I was the moss winding around you
softly always reaching -
higher and higher
to share the view.

But you did not wish to share the view with me
so now all I feel is the forest floor and
the distance between us
as I watch you
growing towards the sun
you never shared with me.

Always on two opposite sides
I filled you with shame
always afraid those around you
would never approve of me
for reasons I still don't know.

So you hid me away
from everyone you could.

While I held you so close,
to wrap myself over you
wanting no harm to find you
as if I where a shield.

Because for all your faults
and all your flaws
no greater man
had I ever loved.

I've spoken only a language I could speak
since always.
Spent all my days searching for people
who knew even a phrase
but no one ever did.

Till you came along and spoke to me
in the same tongue
and suddenly all my loneliness fell away.

I was not one of one but one of two
together the dream grew
of how beautiful it would be
for one and one to make more
who all spoke as we.

Far from perfect from the start
this love of us
and the color it painted the world.

Together, all the battles we fought seemed to make sense
because each battle was won to bring me to you
and each battle lost had led you to me.

Even when you set fire to the care I gave
and sent me away,
I still loved you above all others
tried to balance what I knew with what I hoped.

Till your claws sank so deep within me
I froze
then found flight dashing away
leaving behind
the love language I'd spoken with you.

Rob me of my joy,
only you know the truth
brought me here to take
everything I once held dear
ridiculing me for all I am
taking away the sun in my soul.

Being "honest" just to knock me down,
all I am is not enough,
in spite of all you claim
love for me is your "motivation",
emotional "immaturity" is my new name,
you'll never see your cruel ways.

Just wish you'd let me be free - *Rid of you?*
Nah, you'll never let me.

Laurel Canyon
always felt like a portal
between your world and mine.

Each stop light
a gate asking if we dare
go further
and we always did.

You stealing glances at me
as I played with my hair,
your hand on my thigh
clinging to me,
so I couldn't try to runaway
again.

Sometimes now as I drive that road,
with someone new,
I search for the traces of
that portal,
as if finding it will remind me
that you had been real.

A reminder that you weren't a dream
so I can remember it as it truly was
your beauty when you picked me up
and your ugliness when you brought me
"home."

My perfume no longer smells like me.

It smells like stiff white hotel pillow cases
your blue striped sweater
when I spray it to my skin
it smell like being wrapped in your arms
for the first time
sleepy kisses on my neck.

I wonder how hard you tried not to think of me on my birthday.

How hard was it to hold yourself back from reaching out to anyone who
could have told you how I was?
Did you look me up in hopes of seeing something - anything that might
relieve what you felt inside ?
Perhaps you tried to go on a date with someone new or call up an old
reliable that you would always claim you didn't keep around.

Either way I know the only pieces of you that ever mattered missed me.

Still the only parts of me you ever claimed to know
hope you made every wrong turn home
on that day because you were so consumed by memories of me.

Once you sat
hand wrapped in mine
to slow down
how angry you had been
tears flowing like a river
after the winter thaw.

Your voice but a whisper
so soft as if you didn't even
want the air to hear
"You are so good at loving me
And I have no clue how to love you.
How to be good at it."

I tried to sooth you
and soften the truth
of those words.

Till two months later,
your anger with me
got the better of you again
as I sat crying on the bed
so you looked at me and said
"I'm too old to have to teach someone how to love.
I deserve more than that."

I'm not sure my heart has known
how to love another since.

The gaps seem to be growing wider
but not wide enough for me.

I want the space between who I was with you
and who I am now to be so vast
you can never dream of crossing it.

I want a chasm to form between us
so you can never find
your way back to me.

I remember the first time I actually tried to leave.
The fight had been bad
showing me the cracks a little too clearly,
and one truth from you said it all,
the truth I never could recover from.

It wound its way around my head
taking root deep in the soil of my mind
growing like a rose bush
with thorns and blossoms
that taunted me
each time your love tried to water me.
It was a poison that would lay dormant
then...Every so often...
Even as he lay asleep arms wrapped around me.

These words would come back
and I'd wonder why
why they felt like a siren telling me to get out?
An alarm rushing me to take nothing and go on foot to the hills.
I see it now -
       I hear the words and their cut -
              I get why he spoke them
                    and why I never fully came back to him.

"I'm ashamed of you.
I told her how mature you are how you are
the first intelligent girl I've dated
even though I lived with her - loved her first -
and now -
you are behaving like this?
I'm so embarassed by the way I spoke
thinking you were my equal
when you behave like a child."

Forgetting.
That would be so nice.
but forgetting would take all of it.
Each tiny drop.
Stopping the waves of remembering
that take over my days.
How could I overlook so much?
The first, second, and third time you did those things?
Which was the worst?
My body is bad at keeping the score.

I can't seem to forget any of it.

Because what if it takes something beautiful?

Like my aunt's laugh at thanksgiving
when you were there?
Or my mother's arms so warm around me on my birthday ?
Or the story my father told you at Johnny's that I never heard before?
Or any of the other millions of precious moments I begged you to be a part
of?

I cannot part with those.

So to keep the good
I must keep
the terror and veiled attacks.

Is God not so funny for this?
Perhaps, someday I'll respect them
for making me this way.

Never Could Decide

I think there was a time
when you had hoped
it would be me.

When you let me in
and saw something you haven't seen,
showed parts of yourself
you'd been scared of before.

But when you found
not all would be taken
that easily.

That my own life, humanity, and wellbeing
Had to co-exist with yours,
That future you dreamed of sharing died.

(I couldn't live up to the girl
who lived in your head)

So you never could decide how you felt about me

One day, my youth was so fresh and free
the next I was too young and always needed to learn from you

Sometimes, you liked how I spent my time
but most days you decided
my calendar was never full enough -
(things I did never *meaningful* enough for you)

You didn't like me out in public
I was always too shy
(But also too chatty)

I was so bright and got attention
but never the right kind cus I wasn't a flirt

You hated that I felt feelings outside of you
but got mad that I was prone to shutting down
and shutting you out because

I was never your only puppet

The sex was good but you made sure to let me know you'd had better
and also remind me it was only good because you made it good
(not me)

My beauty was good enough for you
(if you weren't mad at me then -
I was ugly like your ex)

But your friends didn't find me hot enough
to want to fuck behind your back
so that was my problem too
(I still don't understand this one)

I was too old for my dreams
(But too young to be a mother for your kids)
and both were a deep point of
frustration for you and your long term plans.

If you asked me how I feel
it would depend on
the moment you ask
what current thought
fills my head…

I feel as if I'm lost in time
a glitch in the system
because not all of me is in any one place
anymore.

I'm scattered throughout the past,
reaching for magic and moments
I long since know have past.

I keep finding myself driving by old places
as if it can resurrect a love
I'm not even sure I want,
anymore.

And perhaps I'm "okay"
because I get through the day,
but none of me has felt
fine or good or happy
in such a long time.
It feels as if June two summers ago
ate my heart out of my chest.

Once you had been so clear
so smart
knowing you had time on your side
you never let your mask slide
always bribing me to win me
back when my terror filled your room.

But 3 months had passed
and my mind was growing clear again
putting together reality without
your meddling
I had experts now guiding me

3 months for you had only made you
feel all the more cocky and bold
you'd won me back before
in that same amount of time

So you wasted no time -
                    so eager for -
                            what I do not know
But in your quest
you had decided to accept my no as a yes
and when I felt my body bruise
from your attack
I knew at last
there was no more
resurrection
for us.

I'm waiting,
waiting for someone to fill all the space I made
for you but you never bothered to fill
someone who will mean all the words to what
was once our song.
someone who will stay around
long enough to be the road I travel
not just a speed bump along the way.

I'll keep all I learned about myself in the time
I spent beside you
but day by day I'll grant myself
permission to forget what your favorite ice-cream flavor was
and where we had our first kiss
and how it felt when I said I love you
before bed every night.

The gifts you gave me might stay their meaning
long replaced as they just become another
object floating from shelf to shelf.

There is no piece of you
that needs to stay here
when someone new reminds me
I was never
really loved by you.

Time can no longer find me,
My mind rejected it sometime ago,

I float around in fragments

Has it happened yet?

I guess not.

Or maybe it has

I'll struggle to recall
it's the past when I drive past your house
and
expect to get out and
greet you again

I'll float away again
accepting that

I'll only know it when the dream comes true
feel that sensation of the same life
lived twice.

Caught off guard
each time I see photos
from the 4 months
that we had tried again.

The compromise is there in my eyes
and the tight lined "smile"
I wanted you
but you didn't like me as I was
So the deal I tried to make work
was fit for a fable.

A girl who became a ghost
just so she would sit and witness
the life of the man she loved.
If I did not speak
you couldn't get mad
if I did not move you couldn't
blame me.

And in every picture I look back
and see all the ways I tried to be
invisible just so I could keep on
loving you.

To this day there are still moments
when I wonder if I could be that
ghost again, because I still long
to be around that mind I love
in spite of the pain it inflicted.

I know there is no going back
no way to stay safe around you.
so I sit behind my iron walls
ready to breathe fire
should you ever try me again.

In moments I swear
you loved me
when you'd hide in corners
never jumping out to scare me
just waiting like a little boy
for me to come and find you.

Or when you'd get me my favorite snack
or have to play a song
you knew I secretly liked to sing.

How you'd care for my body when it broke down
and love all the pieces of me
that had never seen the light of day

All of these hopes and dreams
of a life with me
I do believe
you once had meant
because even after
you turned on me

I still dream in the night
of the children we had named.

I felt dead after
A ghost of myself
Haunting my life
Going through the motions
Any living version of me would

But I had left my body again
What was the point of staying
In it when others who so
Readily told me they loved me
Would try to take it for their own pleasure.

In daytime and in nightmares alike
When my body found me I'd remember
Both your unwanted touch
And the phone call after
The ice in your voice
Deception finally dropped
The way you - without blinking
Met my most broken self
With a repetition of
Your cruelty.

I remember begging you after betrayal
For some kindness
And all the venom you spat at me
Instead

You hung up
And then I knew

All the love we had shared
Had only ever lived in me
And now both were
dead.

From time to time,
(Even when I know better)
I'll wonder if
I could have done it differently,

Would it have made a difference ?

Was there anyway to correct
or change
the way you only loved me
when I lived up to the fiction
you created?

Maybe, if I was better at
molding myself into the roles
people wanted me to play
I could have stayed

But I've never been good at
saying the words assigned to me
if I don't believe them,
and my temper
hard to rein in,
when I know the truth
is going unsaid.

Still I had tried to be forgiving
and cover your tracks
with lies of my own
to those who saw through you
faster than I had.

Did you ever have a plan?
A plan beyond that afternoon and what you planned to do?

Why was it so important to you
that my no's and stops meant nothing,
that even when I lay there in your bed stiff
unmoving eyes open you kept going?

Was it because you had hoped I wouldn't leave again?
this was the back door way into my life?

That I would take back my vows to never get close to you?

Or was it just because for some reason you wanted the high that comes with
me giving up?

That I would yet again let you get what you wanted even if it might destroy
me?

Is that the proof of unconditional love you always wanted from me?

Or was it just that masturbation had gotten so boring you didn't care what it
took
" To mix it up."

Sometimes I'm grateful not to know why you did it
other-times I wish I knew so I could stop anyone else
I love from doing it again.

Someday,
you'll "fall in love again"
convince some new wide eyed girl
that you are a knight in shining armor
the last good man
you'll be all the things I loved about you
and more for her.

And part of me hopes that's true,
hopes that some of my pain will spare another
that maybe, just maybe,
I was the last stop
on your journey
of cruelty and ultimately
violence.

I know it's wishful thinking to believe
that perhaps maybe I was the only one
you ever treated this way.

As painful as it might be
for the part of me
who only ever wanted
your love, your approval -
Lastly your mercy
to see you "move on"
I pray for the self who will see the signs
and long to throw myself in the line of fire
to try and save
another girl from you.

Justice is a lie

A pipe dream we invented when in our infantile minds we could envision a world better than the one we inhabit.

But there is no justice for women like me.
Who "get played" as they say.

Played by players who's only sport is domination and violence.
Those who get off on the notion that they could make us do with our bodies the very thing we said no to.
If at first we do not desire them they will make us.

There is no justice against men who's winning smiles flash across T.V. screens near and far. Who hide behind their good guy personas and all the women they befriend to cover their tracks.

This kind of player never stops playing.

No relationship is real. It's all pretend. Don't believe me?
You'll see it in the end when he gives you no choice as he holds you to the bed.

There is no justice after
when they still hold the power.

They ensure we who have been violated stay silent by always reminding us the damage they could do.
No more jobs
No friends
No safety at night in our own residence.

There is no justice waiting for me in silence or screams.

My body must find ways to make the nightmares that now live within it, home.
While he keeps wining over new victims and I debate leaving town for good.

It's through this lack of justice I find the reason why mankind invented hell
A place to believe would at last burn him the way I burn daily.

If not justice in this life grant me justice in death
May he face a hell not of heat and fury but frozen abandonment.

This is the cruel prayer I recite
A merging of all parts of the grief I feel for myself and the life before his cruel ways
Anger feels like my only friend since justice never really exists when it's a he said she said.

The results
seemed to take
so long

I watched my own body
like a hawk
trying to decode
every little thing
to ensure
you hadn't done
even more damage
to my body.

I read the medical
cypher in slow motion
taking it word by word
to be sure
thank god I'm in the clear

Perhaps I only got one miracle
in this but I guess I'll be grateful
none the less
to have one less battle
from this to fight.

Living in denial
was such an easy thing to do
feeling I'd stepped out of the loop
played a sly trick
and won.

Till the game caught up to me
his heart on the line
and mine still frozen in time.
Another's hand still wrapped around my throat
as he withholds my breath,
Trying to play at a dream life
with his hand in mine.

But I'm not ready for this love
I'm not ready for any love
that lives beyond the ghost
I made of myself

So I'll set him free
and let time finally
catch up with me.

During these days of you
I've said so many goodbyes

Some long overdue
others I don't think
I'll ever be ready for.

Someday
I'll be better than I am now
no longer the numb
'one getting by
because her check list
tells her to

And when I am
back to myself
I'll get coffee
and apologize
to all those
I've accidentally
let get caught
in your crossfire.   ·

The rest I'll learn to let go.

They Won't Tell Us

They tell us only the weak
get abused
they create an air of shame
to keep us silent.

Tell us only girls with daddy problems
get raped
so we won't tell our families the truth.

They tell us only those who do not love themselves
stay when he grows sour
So we doubt ourselves and never share the stories.

When truthfully we could all be abused
strong, confident, loving, and amusing
can get sucked into a slow dark game
played by a man who's already won it
six times over
sometimes his game goes like this

He plays his little violin,
Exploiting the kindness first
Then he isolates
And sharpens the attacks
Till your head spins
And you can't tell his lies
From your truths
And somehow
Now you're the bad guy
Who needs to make the amends
For not accepting his cruelty

And don't forget the monster in the room is always you
For not knowing he didn't mean to do
It was just his trauma
You remind him of his mama
If you'd stop doing that
Maybe he wouldn't hate you the same way he hates her
Maybe then he wouldn't hurt you the way he hurts her

And when you react and cut through the bullshit
Then it's your trauma overacting
He claims he didn't do it
Till your bags are packed and your heading for the stairs
Now he begs you to stay through tears and stories of ex's upon ex's who did him wrong
Claims he understands the hurt you feel better than anyone
Sharpens the word "I love you"
till it feels like glass under your feet as you try to flee

So you stay
Because you don't know how to leave
He'll wait a few days
And say the problem is your friends

So you'll try to fake making amends
Because this life is a tornado
And you're just along for the ride
Can't even recall what a good nights sleep feels like
Maybe if you play by the rules
He'll let you dream in peace again
Like you did in the beginning

You see I was strong
I loved my life -
My friends, my body, my family, my hobbies, my pets, my past relationships,
I loved damn near every part of being me.

I thought I had done all a woman could
to stay safe.
Still he found his ways to abuse me

I loved both me and him,
I pushed back each step of the way
even when I couldn't leave

Even when he tried to make me hate all I wrote and make me
hate my body,
hate my mind
hate my past,
my heart.

I still found scraps of me he couldn't look deep enough to take
and I fought to keep them safe.

Till he let me get away.

He knew my history
he choose to repeat it.

I was not weak,
I was not a slut
I was a human.
and that's all it took.

That's what they won't tell us.

The strangeness lingers
humming in the background

I'm "moving on" with my life
but it still hurts me to see
the tribe of women
who believe your lies
convinced that you are
"One of the good guys".

I have to remind myself
I once thought you were that person too.
How much heartbreak it took for me to
accept you were never truly the man I thought I met.

There is an anger I think
because I won't let myself feel sad
about each friend I lost
either because they gave up on trying
to save me from you
Or because they believed your lies.

I try to find comfort in my words on the page
the release of the grief I feel
after another the late night confessional
with other women who know this pain.

We sit and talk
till we are no longer numb
and pour out the pain -

                    rage, grief, betrayal, lost love and sorrow-

The feelings of watching lives go on
while ours is forever stopping and starting
half here and half there
and always longing to go back to the before.

But there is no going back, now.
All we can do is make a pact
and promise to be each others safety
even when we know we can't always do that.

I don't mourn you anymore
but grief still sits beside me
her presence is neither
welcome nor unwelcome
just a reminder that
all the love I once felt for you
has no place to call home.

Case Study 04:
New Growth

(Who I am after)

After every fire the forest is born new again.
the miracle of regrowth is even more
meaningful than the first generation.

It's hard not to feel silly
for loving you as deeply
as I did.

I work hard not to carry shame
for all that took place.

It's not an easy process
it's taken me almost a year
to be able to gain some sense
of mental clarity again
I don't feel it everyday
and some hours seem a lifetime.

Nightmares built on my memories
still ebb and flow
but I'm breathing through them
learning how to be more tender to myself
in the days after they reappear.

I've learned not to rely only on myself
to ask for help and not feel like a failure for it
I let myself speak to the love I once felt
I let myself speak to the emptiness that has taken its place
I allow softness and openness without
self judgement.

Being strong comes in so many forms
and this is my version of strong
for now.

"I'll never be who I was before"-

- That doesn't ring true
because every version of me
that I've ever been is
still somehow
someway with me

I might not make the same choices
she would have made
I might know more than she did
and want more than she could

Still, I know if I ever need her
she is still here within me
ready for me to call on her again
should I ever need to.

Blank pages lay before me
Smell of coffee making me nostalgic

For far faded days
the days of paper dolls and pirate ships,
grass stained dresses and octopus de-tangler bottles

I feel closer to these faded memories now
even if they have grown tattered around the edges

I feel like I am her again
she was hopeful, imaginative, and easily loving
there was such a quiet wildness to her mind

Sitting alone wanting to fill this blank page with something I can only hope
will be rendered meaningful I find myself instead reaching -
backwards toward the girl I used to be
who I feel I might have a chance to be again
A fresh start...

A safe space to regrow with my own body if
I water the seeds of nostalgia longing
to nestle down into me

This glimmering little hope calls out to me
and wakens the long sleeping dragon of self
long ago exiled by the shame others
so sweetly pushed forth upon me.
The soft stirring I hope will lead to an
awaking be it meaningful or not
at least it shall be my own.

I put the measuring stick away
the one used to rank me
along side my peers

I accept where I'm at
as just a temporary fact
it's open to change
up for renegotiation
(*someday*)

But for now
it has only been 9 months
since you broke my heart
and 6 since months you broke my consent

It's okay if I'm not all better yet
even when I get angry that
I no longer enjoy hugs
or the feeling of my hand being held

If the only time I feel a rush similar to that
is in dance class with blistered heels
on hikes with the sun blazing over head
or in the blinding stage lights
or with my cat pressed to my side.

It's okay if my loved one's touch
no longer comforts me

I found more peace in seeing myself as I am
then trying to be
just like she used to be.

I can feel the garden growing in my heart again
the flowers I call *Me* are reaching up
towards the sun I know as joy

Love that once only found its home
in your hands has returned to me

at last

Remaking all that I am into a home
in which it can now thrive.

Clarity -
I'm afraid I do not have words to explain to the
onlooker the current state I am in
or what lays beyond today's sunset.

It is spring in my mind.
No thoughts of summer
or the fall harvest
enter my conscious.

What comes of this growth I do not know
all I have in my hands now
is the feeling of reaching and rising
yet again wild and reckless
Seeing to see
no longer caring if I am seen
by others in my natural state.
I spin and dance and sing
and welcome the moment as it is
with only a sense of wonder filling my plate.

There are still moments of doubt
as the weeds he spread through
my mind come up and make me
want to hide from the life
I seek.

It's not always easy to part
with the way I once held
so dearly to him
or the views he shared

He saw me more true than
anyone I'd known
but how he used that
so willingly
to be the most
cruel of the people I've known
isn't always easy to part with.

So on unsuspecting days
when those I admire
speak my praise
wanting nothing from me
not even a scrap
tears sting my eyes
and I hold tight to the
reminders
that there is so much life
left for me and my dreams
now that I'm free.

I thought the Christmas you broke my heart
would be the worst of my life.
An annual anniversary
of the love I lost.
There is no snow
in these San Fernando Hills.
but the holidays still are here.

I miss you for a day
and try to keep it to myself.

It's not easy for many
to understand how I could
miss you or that version of me
that belonged to your whims.
Especially when I'm not really clear
on what it is I miss, anymore.

Because deep down I know
if I had a Christmas wish this year,
it wouldn't be the same as last
when all I wanted was for you to stay.

If I had a wish this year
it wouldn't be a wish at all
but a message of gratitude
to whoever watches from above
for giving me this life back
when they took you away
that December.

Happier without you
and it doesn't make me feel sad
to know this is a fact.

My life is right without you
and that doesn't make me prideful.
I like myself more now that we no longer speak
and that doesn't make me hate you -
though maybe it should.

I work on accepting without feeling
attachment that these are the facts.
they are neither good nor bad.
They just are.

I am neither good nor bad,
for how I pushed back
when I didn't know
how to survive,
I did what was
needed to survive

And sometimes that's enough.

Suffer with me
or
Suffer without me.

It makes no difference
which path you choose
for I truly can not suffer
as you might.

So long as I remember that
the sun will keep rising overhead
the ocean will still greet the shore
and the breeze will always find the trees,

    and
        I get to keep me
            for all my days.

I've spent a lifetime learning
to be grateful to have a chance
to love this body.

To appreciate
all the different ways
there are to feel alive
in this body unique to me.

To remember it was
made for me
and me alone.

Each day I try to be grateful
That I'm the one
who can give care to
this heart of mine.
I'm grateful to live
At the merging of
Ordinary and extraordinary
Because both exist within me.

I think -
I forgot so much of what the mountain peaks taught me.
the lessons learned during the long
sunny winters and starry summers
the things I learned from the people
who now float above me in the beyond
those who loved me before I had
a title, a credit, an address or any status
the love I received as me.

I missed out on so much of my life and joy trying to chase achievements
that would help others see me as the person I knew myself.

I had been loved as my full self before - even if they didn't understand me.

I had so long ago forgotten what it was like to fall asleep without feeling
disappointed in myself for not doing more.
Tying my productivity to every fiber of my being.
Remembering the joys of just sitting on a swing
And singing with the birds? Of timing my breathing to the falling snow?
Looking back I think that my truest self is in those moments.
Is even more the core of me than the creations that fill my spirit. Perhaps
because each thing I make is born from the gifts only my own peace can
grant me.

Someone's Someone

Benevolent,
tender,
funny,
so handsome he should be carved in stone,

Spending his days building a future,
to provide, protect and care for the family
he plans to make.

Closing my eyes I can see it all so clearly
the Christmas mornings
and Easter dinners,
the high school graduations
and senior home birthday parties
with him always shining at the center.

I look at him and can see it all so clearly
the picturesque future
won't be just a picture

I know he is someone's someone
their whole world shines in his
playful brown eyes

But he isn't mine.
and I'm not his.

Our hearts belong to someone
we haven't quite yet met
but, how lovely it is to spend this time together
to take care of someone's someone.
while we wait for our soulmates.

This feels lighter
than all the love
I've felt before.

This one might not last
much longer
but for once I don't mind.

I only feel grateful
that our trains passed by in the night
of this life.

It started off slow.
like it always does.

A spontaneous risk.
A shot in the dark.
I met you half way.

You liked how it felt.
So you tried it again.
And again.
And again.

Till we both felt it grow.
A string being pulled.
Till one day

I grew brave and I asked
"Why? "

You replied:

"My day is better with the sound of your voice"
So every other day I speak for 30 minutes there and 30 minutes back.
Everything and nothing about my world fills the space while you drive.
Between my words and your breaths we can pretend it's safe to love each
other again -
if only through the phone .

I like making choices
for myself.

Getting to decide what I make
without fear of failing
because I'm no longer living
to please someone else.

I think that is the truth of
"Inner Child" work -
going back to a time
when I did not consume
the fear of others
and retrofit myself
so they would be comfortable.

I'm wearing the clothes
that make me feel something.

Deciding on a whim.

I'm making the kind of jokes that make me laugh
writing poems that make me feel
and painting the world I want look at.

I am forgetting and unlearning
every criticism that was spoken to stop me in my tracks
and I'm learning gratitude for the feedback
that helped me discover new ways to try.

I embrace the joy
of no longer creating
under anyone's thumb.

Lazy summer days
that often pass others by
linger deep within me.

Dripping slowly into my being
like honey thick with
crystals at the bottom.

In the room I pretend to do
many a thing
when in reality
I lay and mull
the tender feelings
of my own lungs
rising and falling
with each serene breath.

I'm not sure
what to call this season
it's not a time of new growth
it's not wild or untamed
nor is it a time of weeding down and releasing.

Perhaps it is a time of deepening.
Of reaching down into the depths of what
I have always known and sinking so far down
into the earth that I can no longer hear the
unnecessary comments of others
so that the only sound I hear
is the sound of my own inner knowing.

It feels nice
to laugh again.

No,
it feels better than nice to find these
pockets where I am breathing through the night
to let myself talk, and dance, and sing along,
without trying to watch myself through
someone else's eyes to ensure I pass the
"good enough test."

I enjoy not being good enough at this human thing.

I like being part princess and part dragon.
Making flower crowns I might accidentally rip
with my clumsy claws.

I like giving myself permission to write fantasy
words in my poems
to know I am no less a grown woman
for my whimsy.

That pain and fairy dust are a part of the mix
just like sugar and spice
and paint and pen.

A second chance
not at love but
for something else
awaits me in this
warm coffee shop.

I sit hopeful
that amends
can be made
when I explain
who I was last summer
and the choices I made.

Though I won't call him by name
but I hope you'll understand
so I can
put forth
the suggestion

A nudge at friendship
now we are a year removed
is an option worth
your consideration.

6 months into the year.
And July brings many things with it.
This me that was once just a concept has
started to take form.
She is calling the shots and slowly
making herself known to the world.

I like her.
Each step forward she takes
shapes, creates and plows a new path all of
her own making.
Leading the way and letting the world
fill in the gaps as we go.

I find that this is exciting.
This was what has not so secretly
been longed for.
Even if I have no idea where
she is taking me and if we shall succeed.

I know this path
and person is worth more to me
than the life I called mine
6 months ago.

Even if this is the end
of the story
I once called us
and there is no epilogue
to help us cheat death,
I believe that we were meant to find each other.

Just like I believe we were meant
to lose each other.

The blazing daylight
ready to burn it all down
set fire to me
If it meant reaching your ends
and my frosted moonlight so
willing to freeze you out
the moment our desires no longer intertwined -

Yes, we were meant to meet.
We were meant to part.

Night and Day never
stay lingering together long
no matter how beautiful
the colors we made.

In a place beyond
the one we are waking in
there is a river running
wisdom of a different nature
stretches out along the river banks,
always timeless in this true realm.

In this sacred stream
that first watered the physical seed
I place the illusion of my hands within,
I watch the ripples reach me
as two golden fish swim
over palms and fingers.

Their message is simple
but not known at first.
Still it finds me when the time is right
and my mind no longer one with the flood.

Ancestors guide me
back.

Rising up out of my core
steady at first
just a warm glow
till it swells and expands
then like fireworks
launches off and spreads
through my whole body
igniting each nerve
with that long awaited for feeling.

One I am not second guessing.

I know at last *happiness* has returned.

Two opposites live within me at once
sorrow shaking me so I dare not move,
and joy so full I can't help but dance.

With each day I am
spun between the two
as I heal wounds
I once grounded in
and find the happinesses in what I once avoided.

Duality is the scariest of experiences
but hope is growing somehow
between the two.

I didn't realize
when the first text was sent
just how close the universe had drawn
our life lines.

I thought I was doing simple favor at best
never knew the gift I had been sent

I had found another just like me

The horror we went through
almost the same
Two different faces but their souls the same
we shared these parts of the same story
Same heart,
Same lover,
Same monster,

How could it be?
We were asked.

Why did you stay
We were shamed.

It made no sense to all my friends
who had never had their own Jekyll and Hyde
the man who was once their best friend

But to her it made sense
and with her I was safe
in ways I hadn't been
since I'd let myself fall in love
with him.

Come join me as you are,
reach with me beyond,
the limits of what they
tell us is so.

Let us find the limits,
of the universe as
it is known,
and push

          push

              push.

till the limits give way.
Leaving only the rush of
our new explorations beyond.

I thought that losing him
would create a gap in connection
I couldn't fill
I settled
stayed
gave in
and accepted the unacceptable
because I was afraid of the truth I'd find in
solitude
any connection was better than no connection.

In losing him I lost something that only carried meaning because I gave it
meaning.
It only held life because I breathed life into it.
It was laced with love because I scarified my heart for it.

But I gained
a community of women who left.
Escaped or pushed for what's right till they were set free.

During the cocoon phase we sat together
raged
cried
laughed
and awoke a new.

This path isn't easy
these memories are haunting
and the healing might be a life long act
but it's not one I'll ever face alone

thank you to my warriors

The horizon line ignites
a tapestry of warm hues
breaking the black of night
welcoming a new dawn.

I stand on the mountain's ledge
feeling a rush
not known since
the wildest days of childhood
I am alone
a stark contrasted spot on the skyline

Yet here in this moment
I am the dawn
the breeze
the rushing water
the rocky mountains beneath my feet.

I am alive.

I am life.

EPILOGUE

You are not alone.

Even when you feel you are.

When your world feels as if it is crashing and your own mind no longer feels safe.
When every breath feels scary and you can't seem to outrun all the things that chew on your bones.

Please remember there are people out there who know.
Perhaps not him who has hurt you, but who those know their own monsters. Who understand what it was like to love someone who is cruel. Who will never question nor mock all the times you went back. Those will never think you stupid or weak or naive for loving someone through the attacks.

I learned how to breathe again.
How to sleep through the nights.
When I learned not to fear asking for reminders of love from those who braved this before me.

Acknowledgements

No man is an island and *it takes a village* is an understatement.

This book is born from the labor of love, that is at times, loving me. Who knew so many big feelings could fit in someone so little?

So first things first, I'm so grateful for my family. Especially my parents. I don't know how I got so lucky as to have two parents who always saw me for who I was, and grant me the freedom to be her.
They still make endless sacrifices everyday because they believe in not only me but what I create. This book and so much of my healing is thanks to them.
To my sister thank you, for making me feel better each and every time I felt my world was ending. For always understanding when I didn't want a hug, and for all do you to help me create.
To all the countless friends and loved ones who indulge in my rambles over coffee, 2am chains of spam texts, who showed up for my readings, various shows, and most of all always seeing the human in me, and the best in me, at the same time.
Thank you to all the beautiful people who have been through their own journeys through *The In-Between.* Each of you are the knights of shining armor in my life for your acts of vulnerability by telling me your stories so I'd find the strength to tell mine.
And last but most definitely not least thank you to every kind stranger who has found my words one way or another and had the courage to share their stories with me. Your words remind me why creations are meant to be shared even if it scares me shitless.
I hope that even one of these poems has helped you to feel a little more understood.

Thank you all so much.

- Noëlle

About The Author

Noelle Cope is an actress, screenwriter, and poet.

Originally born in the snowy mountains and high altitude of Telluride, Colorado where a wild spirit was ingrained from the start. Along with a deep love of storytelling.
At 7 years old Noelle made her first attempt at writing a novel.
Then at 9 announced her desire to be an actress, which was followed, by her first screenplay at age 11.
Thanks to the support these humble beginnings received, she wound up moving to Los Angeles, CA in her teen years with her family.
As an actress she has lent her voice to shows for Netflix, Hulu, and Amazon Prime.
As screenwriter she co-wrote the film *Snow Angels* with Taylor Blackwell.

Notes From The In-between is her debut poetry collection.

If you wish to learn more about Noelle you can find her on instagram and other social media platforms @noellacope

Or sign up for her substack 26 Letters By Noelle